Perry The Inventor's®
WORLD'S BEST SELLING
TIME BLOCKING
PLANNER

A Simple and Effective Tool To Plan and Conquer Your Biggest Goals Through Time Blocking

Use this planner to do great things. Any idiot can post images of what they eat or complain or troll. You, my brilliant friend, are a goal setting productive person bound to do great things. You have bigger goals and dreams. This planner is made to help you focus on creating real positive change for yowurself and the rest of us. Go boldly into the world and do great things!

For BULK orders or to learn more about other Perry The Inventor® Products contact us...
Sales@PerryTheInventor.com
http://PerryTheInventor.com

We offer training and speaking on the following topics...
inNOWvation™:   Rapid Ideation Techniques To Invent Cool Now.
Entrepreneurship: Inventing Profits
Leadership Through Innovation
and more...

What Amazing People Are Saying

"I knew there was something special about Perry the moment I met him. He has a fascinating way of looking at the world that allows him come up with the most innovative ideas I've ever seen. But what's most impressive is his genuine desire to help others and see them happy. I hold him in the highest regard as an inventor, businessman and friend."
Pablo Rosario
Program Director of The Society International

"Perry the inventor is one of the most innovative, creative people I know. He is a joy to work with and has an infectious enthusiasm that comes through his businesses, writing, and designs."
Justin Gary
Award Winning Game Designer and CEO

"The way Perry taught me to think about problem solving and innovation has changed how I approach everything from writing a work email to cleaning my house. At a minimum I find myself asking two to three times a week 'What would Perry say? How would Perry re-frame this?'"
Nathan Riehl
Entrepreneur and Inspiring Philosopher

"Perry the Inventor is an amazingly innovative thinker and generous with his advice and experience. I'm proud to count him as a mentor and a friend."
David Nguyen
Founder ThruGreen.com

"Perry The Inventor changed the way I see the universe by injecting the essence of a creative inventive mindset directly into my cerebral cortex. Fortunes are spent trying to bottle what he freely gives, a fountain of youth obtained by having a child-like courage to face the world."
Chris Jordan
Master Sales Guru, ChrisJordan.co

"Perry lets his imagination free with a sense of endless creativity that is not only fast-paced, but also adventurous. His support and knowledge of the patent product invention world is invaluable and greatly influence the development of my own products!"
Joshua Fischbach
Entrepreneur & businessman, Founder The Best Coffee in the Universe INC.

"Perry is the inventor, thinker and all around passionate guy who, by just interacting with him, infects you with a joy and excitement for looking at new possibilities and turning them into opportunities."
Anthony Peters
The Science Based Hypnotist, Neuronosis.com

"Perry The Inventor is a trusted personal friend that can be counted on for a myriad of support from technical to entrepreneurial to relationships. His sage advice, opinions and creative ideas are often sought after and always valuable."
Joseph Moore, CEO AEB Technologies

"Perry is creative, talented and hard working. I wish their were more genuine people like Perry!"
Heidi Larson, HB's Toys & Accessories LLC

"Perry is my go-to guy for ancient secret wisdom on all things patent-and-invention related!"
Crockett Dunn, Founder/CEO Crockett Dunn LLC

To Teri, my loving wife and best friend.

The only person who can make time stop simply by holding my hand.

Table of Contents

Section One

Why This Book Now?

Because To Do Lists Must Die!

I've struggled with to-do lists my entire life. In theory, they're brilliant. In reality, they're torture. As a time management tool, I hate to-do lists.

Why? Because they quickly fill with garbage-tasks and are endless. True, the concept of the to-do list is simple. You write your tasks, prioritize them and get to work. "Tick completed tasks with a red-pen to feel better psychologically," a consultant once told me. But soon you are overwhelmed. There are always more to-dos and a constant horrible feeling of never getting enough done.

Endlessly growing to-do lists bothered me. And after deep reflection and reading countless articles on time, task, and project management I had an epiphany. If I schedule tasks they are prioritized and ready to be worked on with time already alloted. Which makes tasks easier to complete.

I realized time is the only constant. You cannot rely on your to-do tasks being correct, but you can depend on 1:00 pm being 1:00 pm. Time is precise, finite and beautiful. To get tasks done, you must schedule them.

And time is a brilliant arbiter. While every little task works its way onto your to-do list, not everything gets on your schedule. Many tasks aren't worth your time. You can delegate or delete many of them. And being stingy with your time increases your productivity. What happens when you schedule your time for your most valuable tasks? Magic!

The second realization I had was one I discovered. While thinking about time, I realized every moment you're alive you're either Creating or Consuming. No judgment here! Consuming the book "Cat's Cradle" by Kurt Vonnegut is a beautiful way to spend your time. If you stop consuming food you'll die. You must consume and also create.

As part of this realization I also discovered that what you create and consume determines your quality of life. It's simple, elegant and powerful. Because you control what you create and consume, you control the quality of your life. You're in charge.

LIFE QUALITY = CREATE + CONSUME

The quality of your life is the result of what you create plus what you consume. It's that easy.

If your daily routine consists of consuming ten fat juicy cheeseburgers and watching (consuming) eight hours of mindless reality TV, at the end of a year what will your life look? If you live, you'll be fat, bored and dull. You might even succumb to a disease like diabetes or have a heart attack.

Why? You're out of balance; too much consuming. And you're consuming negative things. Consuming negative things is dangerous to your health, mind, and body.

So should you switch to being a 100% creator? Should you constantly create as much and as often as possible?

Think about this, what would your life look like if you work 20 hours a day, routinely gulp down fast food, never rest and wholly focus on creating 24/7/365? Believe it or not, you will probably have the same heart attack your consume-heavy life was destined for. Excessive creating and excessive consuming are both bad for you.

Balance and Quality

The trick to the good life is balance and quality. Consume/create positive experiences in appropriate balance. As much as you healthily can. Balance is good.

Everyone knows that quality matters. High-quality food is more nutritious and tastes better than junk. Watching Banksy's "Exit Through the Gift Shop" is more mentally stimulating than seeing which TV Reality Star is having a meltdown this week. Deep down you know quality is what really matters.

Quality is the good/bad value of the creates and consumes in your equation. Consume a nutritious meal? That adds to your life. Consume garbage? That subtracts from your life.

Create something positive, and you enrich your life. Create something negative, and you worsen your life.

You're not looking for a number from this equation. You're looking for a legacy. How people remember you is based on how much greatness you've created and how well you've consumed. And that's in your full control. Pick big goals, schedule the tasks to complete them and go do great things. Become a great person by accomplishing great goals.

And if you're not sure what to do next, just ask yourself, "Right now, what positive things should I be creating or consuming? Am I in balance?"

Once you begin to create and consume good things, in balance, you will see the quality of your life increase. And people will notice. Heck, you'll notice too. You'll probably look better, feel better, have more money and better friends.

Simple Tools Get Used
Next, I learned that simple tools are better than complicated tools. Why? Because simple tools get used. Tools benefit you when you use them.

I discovered Time blocking through an article by Cal Newport on his "Study Hacks Blog". Cal is the person credited with coining the term "Time Blocking". Thanks, Cal!

Essentially, Time Blocking is scheduling your tasks. Scheduling tasks is nothing new. But it is incredible.

Scheduling tasks is as simple as writing a to-do list, but infinitely more powerful and productive. You know what to do when. No more time wasted figuring out which task to do next. You simply work.

Your New BFF
This planner is designed to be your companion for the next year. It has enough pages to map 12 months of time and additional pages for goal planning and notes. Each weekly spread is on

facing pages which enables you to view a full week, all 168 hours, simultaneously. Sweet, right?

All pages are un-dated which means you can begin when you decide. Want to start right now? Go for it!

Start by planning your big yearly goal(s) and schedule when you will complete them.

Monthly Planning pages let you see goals by weeks and in steps. This enables you to focus your attention on what's important.

Weekly planning pages show time slots for 24 hours each day and begin at 5:00 am. Use each time slot to schedule specific tasks. Feel free to use blank spaces for notes.

This planner is great to schedule time and tasks for work, home and yourself. You probably don't want to record every idea here as you'll want more space. I suggest you also buy and use an Innovation Journal to capture your thoughts. Personally, I use two physical books. This one for my time and a different one to capture my ideas.

See the Sample Pages For Ideas
I made sample pages for you. You can get ideas from them but you don't have to follow them. You can use this planner any way you'd like and feel free innovate. Yes, use colored pens and pencils, draw silly images, and remember to have fun. The goal is to map your tasks to your time to increase your productivity and, yes, you can indeed have fun doing that.

Thanks for investing in yourself and this planner. I'm look forward to hearing about your journey! If you have any suggestions, thoughts or comments, please, reach out to me.

Contact me...
Website: PerryTheInventor.com
Email: TimeBlockingPlanner@PerryTheInventor.com
Twitter: @PerryInvents
LinkedIn: LinkedIn.com/In/PerryTheInventor

GOOD
abc MORNING
AMERICA

PERRY

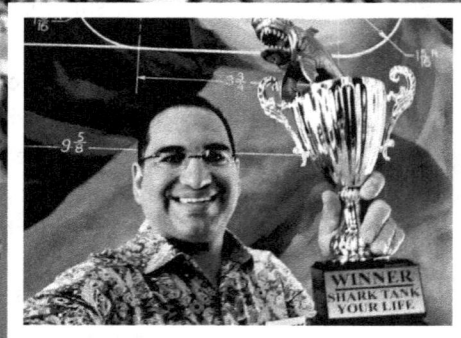

WINNER
SHARK TANK
YOUR LIFE

PERRY

Section Two
Examples

Top: I won Good Morning America's Shark Tank Your Life with my ShapeSHARK invention. A version of it sold Millions.
Bottom: I met Daymond John. He selected me as the ABC GMA Shark Tank Your Life winner.
Center: There I am holding the Cheesy Plastic Trophy which I love; painted plastic shark and all! Great Memories and lots of fun.

Yearly BIG Goals _1/1/2179__

START _____

I am working to achieve this...

I want to license a Product to a Major Company

1. Choose 1-3 MAJOR goals for this year. Select Life changing goals you'd be proud to achieve.
2. Map out the tasks you must complete to succeed.
3. Commit to dates to begin each step.
4. Consider potential obstacles and how to destroy them. You are the Task Terminator and nothing will stop you!
5. Begin! There is magic in beginning!

Time favors the persistent. Everyday move toward your goal. You may have setbacks, you may need to start over. But that is okay because the best goals are worth the effort. And the rewards are worth the work. Begin today. Move toward your goal. And soon you will be celebrating its achievement. Go For Your Goal!

Goal Tasks (Start __1/1/2179_)

Research...
Let's see if I know what I need to know. I will spend the next 4 weeks researching this.

Update: There is lots to learn. I decided to take a course in ideation, prototyping and licensing from PerryTheInventor.com.

(Completed _2/6/2179_)

Goal Tasks (Start _2/14/2179_)

Ideation: I took 3 weeks to ideate and have over two dozen ideas. I used a free Idea Valuation Template from (PerryTheInventor.com/IdeaValue) to see which idea I should work on.

My idea with the best chance of success is my "Rocket Ribs Exerciser." I am excited.

(Completed _3/8/2179_)

Goal Tasks (Start _3/14/2179_)

Prototype: "Rocket Ribs Exerciser" Make a Frankenstein Prototype. (PerryTheInventor.com/Frankenstein)

Update: I made 14 prototypes and mods in the past 6 weeks. The costs was surprisingly cheap as I did it all myself. No need to hire a professional. Really excited.

(Completed _5/1/2179_)

Goal Tasks (Start _5/1/2179_)

Intellectual Property: "Rocket Ribs Exerciser" Checking to see if I can own it.

Update: Got Patent Pending for thousands less than an attorney by doing it myself. It was easier than I thought it would be.

(Completed _6/1/2179_)

SAMPLE * SAMPLE * SAMPLE

Goal Tasks (Start _____)

Completed Task Early. If I needed more steps I could have used more paper. Less steps use less boxes.

(Completed _____)

SUCCESS Achieved _11/29/2179_

Here is how I achieved my goal!
1- Ideate
2- Prototype and Test
3- Check IP   Good = Go
                 Bad = Drop
4 - Costing
5 - Selling / Market Test
6 - License / Sell
I will do another idea ASAP

Goal Tasks (Start _8/9/2179_)

License: "Rocket Ribs Exerciser" License deal.

Update: I had two offers and selected the company that agreed to commit to a larger marketing budget. They love the invention and gave me a sweet advance and a nice royalty.

(Completed _11/29/2179_)

Goal Tasks (Start _8/9/2179_)

License or Manufacture: "Rocket Ribs Exerciser" Exploring Licensing and Manufacturing. Found great article at (PerryTheInventor. com/ShortRun)

Update: Made and sold 10 units. Now I am meeting with manufacturers to discuss licensing.

(Completed _9/4/2179_)

Goal Tasks (Start _6/4/2179_)

Costing: "Rocket Ribs Exerciser" Need $10 cost for home and $100 for Pro. I learned this from the free costing article at (PerryTheInventor.com/ CostingModel).

Update: I found two paths to product. 1) Home Model, 2) Pro Model. Two different models. Will test market each.

(Completed _7/1/2179_)

Goal Tasks (Start 7/14/2179)

Market Test: "Rocket Ribs Exerciser" Testing Home Model at $49 and Pro Model at $499.

Update: Home Model is tough sell. People don't want it because I don't have a celebrity tied to it. But Pro Model is a hit. I have several Gyms who want to order and several personal trainers who want it.

(Completed _8/4/2179_)

SAMPLE * SAMPLE * SAMPLE

Monthly Planning   Month_January_   Year _2179_

	Week 1				Week 2		
Goal 1	**Goal 2**	**Goal 3**		**Goal 1**	**Goal 2**	**Goal 3**	
Exercise Daily	Reorganize Office	Family Dinner 5x This week	1	**LONG PROJECT EXAMPLE** It's your planner use it like you want to!			
Find a Gym	Create Presentation	Plan Menus	2	**Jan 7** Project X For Mr. Big	**SAMPLE * SAMPLE * SAMPLE**		
Join Morning Gym Classes	Sell Boss on Idea	Send invite so everyone is on time	3	Spec Project			
Begin 1/7/2179	Build Team (Call Alice+BG)	Me home by 6pm to cook	4	Assign Team			
	Clear out Old Files		5	**Jan 14** Prototype			
	Get new Label Maker		6	Approval	**Jan 21** Beta		
	Move files to Off-site Archive		7		**Jan 28** Revisions		
	Shred Old Data		8		**Feb 6** Beta 2		
			9		**Feb 12** QA	**Feb 18** Final Fixes	
			10			**Feb 28** Soft Launch	
			11			**Mar 18** Product Review	
SAMPLE * SAMPLE * SAMPLE			12				

Pick 1 - 3 Weekly Goals. These may relate to your yearly goals or may be smaller. Write the goal in step 1 and then the tasks required to complete it. Complete the takes during the week.

Week 3

Goal 1	Goal 2	Goal 3
Learn to Pickle Things	Read "Do Androids Dream of Electric Sheep"	Fix Garage Door
Google Pickling		
Order Mason Jars and Spices		
Add rest of steps once learned		
SAMPLE * SAMPLE * SAMPLE		

1
2
3
4
5
6
7
8
9
10
11
12

Week 4

Goal 1	Goal 2	Goal 3
Read "48 Laws of Power"	Plan Party for Martha's 10 Year of Service	Find new Lawn Service
	Email invitations at work	
	Assign Pot Luck Items	
	Order Cake from Vinola's because Martha loves them	
	Reserve Conference Room	
	SAMPLE * SAMPLE * SAMPLE	

Sunday 1	Monday 2	T	Tuesday 3	Wednesday 4
		5a	WAKE UP	
	WAKE UP	6a	TRAVEL	WAKE UP
	MEDITATION 15		BOARD MEETING	MEDITATION 15
	EXERCISE 30	7a		EXERCISE 30
	SHOWER			SHOWER
	TRAVEL 30M		TRAVEL TO OFFICE	WAFFLE WED
WAKE-UP	AT OFFICE	8a	OFFICE	WITH THE CLUB
MEDITATION 15m	PLAN WEEK		EMAILS + CALLS	EMAILS + CALLS
EXERCISE 30M		9a		
SHOWER				
FLEX TIME	WRITE COPY FOR	10a		
	MARKETING			
		11a	TEAM MEETING	WORK ON PROJECT
				FOR PTI CORP
	LUNCH w/ Mitchell	12p	LUNCH w/ TERi	
	WRITE FOR SOCIAL	1p	TERi PROJECT	LUNCH WITH
	CAMPAIGN AND		GO OVER PROOFS	SHAINA
GROCERY SHOPPING	RESEARCH	2p	CREATIVE	WORK ON PROJECT
APPLES				FOR PTI CORP
SALAD		3p	THINKING	
OLD BAY	EMAILS + CALLS			
PLUS USUAL		4p	TIME	
	PREP FOR TERi			
	MEETING TOMORROW			
Cook + freeze	QA TEAM'S WORK	5p	WRITE-UP REPORT	Review Budgets
MEALS FOR Week	+ PLAN FOR		FOR TERi	
	TEAM MEETING	6p	SITE LAUNCH	Budget meeting
	TOMORROW		WORK	
Family Dinner	SITE LAUNCH	7p	FAMILY DINNER	family Dinner
	WORK			
	FAMILY DINNER	8p	Qigong CLASS	
	READ MY BOOK	9p		
	BED	10p	READ BOOK	Read Book
		11p	BED	BED
	ANDY called: SITE	12p		
	LAUNCH is ON			
	SCHEDULE. DOING	1a		
	FINAL QA THIS			
	Week	2a		
		3a		
		4a		

Thursday 5	Friday 6	T	Saturday 7	Notes
		5a		CHOC.FACTORY 954 8675309
	WAKE UP	6a		Bob's # 954.202.6426
	MEDITATION 15 EXERCISE 30 SHOWER		WAKE UP	
WAKE UP	MASTERMIND GROUP	7a	MEDITATION 15 EXERCISE 30 SHOWER	
MEDITATION 15 EXERCISE 30 SHOWER	APPROVE SITE FOR LAUNCH	8a	Road TRIP	
MARKETING Meeting	EMAILS + CALLS	9a		
EMAIL + CALLS	INVENTING + Prototyping	10a	Visit CHOCOLATE FACTORY	
1 CLIENT COACHING BL 2 CLIENT Coaching TH		11a		
3 CLIENT Coaching NS 4 CLIENT Coaching AA	Lunch	12p		
LUNCH with Nicole	WRITE Proposals	1p		
5 CLIENT Coaching GL	LAUNCH SITE W/ TEAM	2p		
WRITING	CALL CLIENTS To check ON Progress	3p		
		4p	DO ESCAPE ROOM	
INVENTING	INVENTORY + ORDER Supplies	5p		
	FAMILY DINNER	6p		
PROTOTYPING	PACK FOR Road TRIP	7p	DINNER	
Family DINNER AND Game Night		8p	family Game Night	
	Qigong CLASS	9p		
	READ BOOK	10p	Bed	
	BED	11p		
Bed		12p		
		1a		
		2a		
		3a		
		4a		

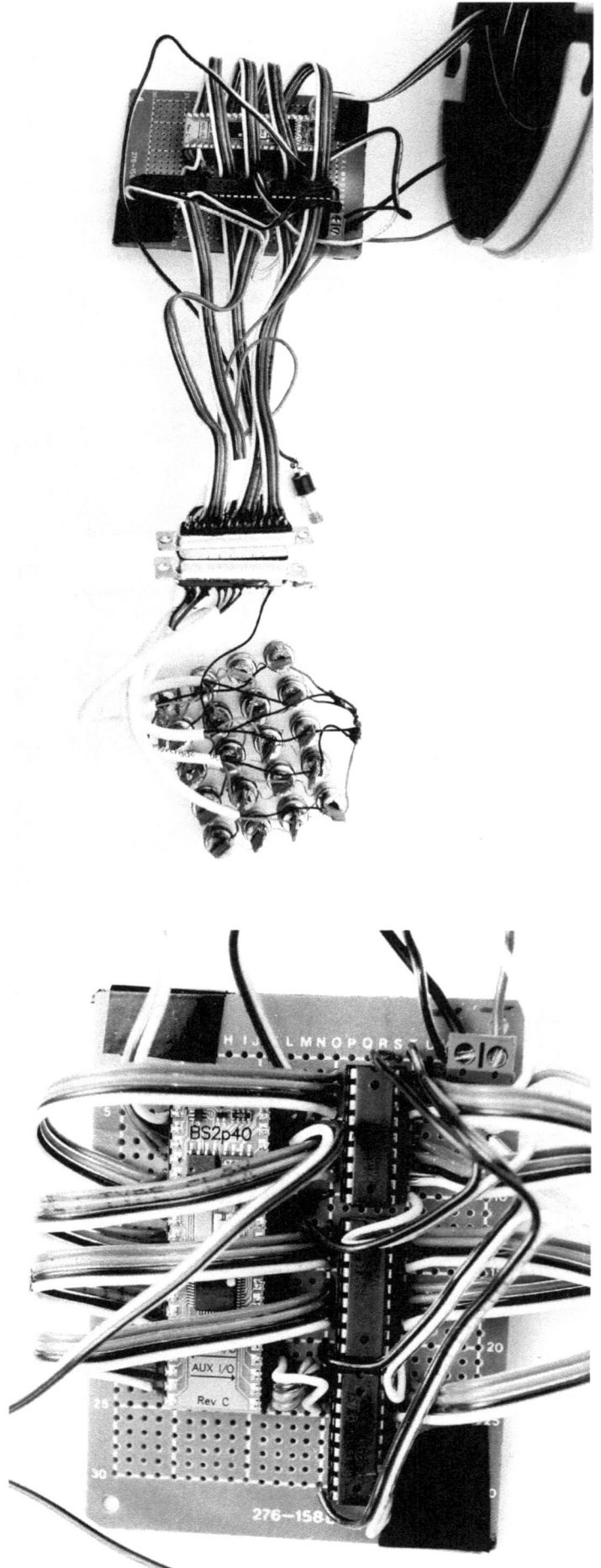

Section Three
Yearly Big Goals Pages

Left: A toy prototype made using an Arduino, a custom PCB and lots of manual soldering. Worked like a charm.
Top Right: A prototype using a Basic Stamp and an array of lasers. It too worked like a charm.
Bottom Right: Close up of hand wired PCB from above.

Yearly BIG Goals _____/_____/_____

START _____

I am working to achieve this...

1. Choose 1-3 MAJOR goals for this year.
Select Life changing goals you'd be proud to achieve.
2. Map out the tasks you must complete to succeed.
3. Commit to dates to begin each step.
4. Consider potential obstacles and how to destroy them.
You are the Task Terminator and nothing will stop you!
5. Begin! There is magic in beginning!

Time favors the persistent. Everyday move toward your goal. You may have setbacks, you may need to start over. But that is okay because the best goals are worth the effort. And the rewards are worth the work. Begin today. Move toward your goal. And soon you will be celebrating its achievement. Go For Your Goal!

Goal Tasks (Start _____)

(Completed _____)

Goal Tasks (Start _____)

(Completed _____)

Goal Tasks (Start _____)

(Completed _____)

Goal Tasks (Start _____)

(Completed _____)

SUCCESS Achieved _____/_____/_____

Goal Tasks (Start _____)

(Completed _____)

Here is how I achieved my goal!

Goal Tasks (Start _____)

Goal Tasks (Start _____)

(Completed _____)

(Completed _____)

Goal Tasks (Start _____)

Goal Tasks (Start _____)

(Completed _____)

(Completed _____)

Yearly BIG Goals _____/_____/_____

START _____

> I am working to achieve this...

1. Choose 1-3 MAJOR goals for this year.
Select Life changing goals you'd be proud to achieve.
2. Map out the tasks you must complete to succeed.
3. Commit to dates to begin each step.
4. Consider potential obstacles and how to destroy them.
You are the Task Terminator and nothing will stop you!
5. Begin! There is magic in beginning!

Time favors the persistent. Everyday move toward your goal. You may have setbacks, you may need to start over. But that is okay because the best goals are worth the effort. And the rewards are worth the work. Begin today. Move toward your goal. And soon you will be celebrating its achievement. Go For Your Goal!

Goal Tasks (Start _____)

(Completed _____)

Goal Tasks (Start _____)

(Completed _____)

Goal Tasks (Start _____)

(Completed _____)

Goal Tasks (Start _____)

(Completed _____)

SUCCESS Achieved _____/_____/_____

Goal Tasks (Start _____)

(Completed _____)

Here is how I achieved my goal!

Goal Tasks (Start _____)

(Completed _____)

Goal Tasks (Start _____)

(Completed _____)

Goal Tasks (Start _____)

(Completed _____)

Goal Tasks (Start _____)

(Completed _____)

Yearly BIG Goals _____ / _____ / _____

START _____

I am working to achieve this...

1. Choose 1-3 MAJOR goals for this year.
Select Life changing goals you'd be proud to achieve.
2. Map out the tasks you must complete to succeed.
3. Commit to dates to begin each step.
4. Consider potential obstacles and how to destroy them.
You are the Task Terminator and nothing will stop you!
5. Begin! There is magic in beginning!

Time favors the persistent. Everyday move toward your goal. You may have setbacks, you may need to start over. But that is okay because the best goals are worth the effort. And the rewards are worth the work. Begin today. Move toward your goal. And soon you will be celebrating its achievement. Go For Your Goal!

Goal Tasks (Start _____)

(Completed _____)

Goal Tasks (Start _____)

(Completed _____)

Goal Tasks (Start _____)

(Completed _____)

Goal Tasks (Start _____)

(Completed _____)

SUCCESS Achieved _____/_____/_____

Goal Tasks (Start _____)

(Completed _____)

Here is how I achieved my goal!

Goal Tasks (Start _____)

(Completed _____)

Goal Tasks (Start _____)

(Completed _____)

Goal Tasks (Start _____)

(Completed _____)

Goal Tasks (Start _____)

(Completed _____)

山辉川媚

Section Four
Time Blocking Pages

Monthly Planning 1   Month _____   Year _____

Week 1				Week 2		
Goal 1	**Goal 2**	**Goal 3**		**Goal 1**	**Goal 2**	**Goal 3**
			1			
			2			
			3			
			4			
			5			
			6			
			7			
			8			
			9			
			10			
			11			
			12			

26   Perry The Inventor's® World's Best Selling Time Blocking Planner

Pick 1 - 3 Weekly Goals. These may relate to your yearly goals or be smaller.
Write the goal in step 1 and then each task required to complete it. Complete tasks during the week.

Week 3				Week 4		
Goal 1	**Goal 2**	**Goal 3**		**Goal 1**	**Goal 2**	**Goal 3**
			1			
			2			
			3			
			4			
			5			
			6			
			7			
			8			
			9			
			10			
			11			
			12			

Sunday ___	Monday ___		Tuesday ___	Wednesday ___
		5a		
		6a		
		7a		
		8a		
		9a		
		10a		
		11a		
		12p		
		1p		
		2p		
		3p		
		4p		
		5p		
		6p		
		7p		
		8p		
		9p		
		10p		
		11p		
		12p		
		1a		
		2a		
		3a		
		4a		

FOCUS 2 _____

Thursday____	Friday____	T	FOCUS 3 _____ Saturday____	Notes
		5a		
		6a		
		7a		
		8a		
		9a		
		10a		
		11a		
		12p		
		1p		
		2p		
		3p		
		4p		
		5p		
		6p		
		7p		
		8p		
		9p		
		10p		
		11p		
		12p		
		1a		
		2a		
		3a		
		4a		

Sunday ___	Monday ___		Tuesday ___	Wednesday ___
		5a		
		6a		
		7a		
		8a		
		9a		
		10a		
		11a		
		12p		
		1p		
		2p		
		3p		
		4p		
		5p		
		6p		
		7p		
		8p		
		9p		
		10p		
		11p		
		12p		
		1a		
		2a		
		3a		
		4a		

FOCUS 2 _____

Thursday_____	Friday_____	T	Saturday_____	Notes
		5a		
		6a		
		7a		
		8a		
		9a		
		10a		
		11a		
		12p		
		1p		
		2p		
		3p		
		4p		
		5p		
		6p		
		7p		
		8p		
		9p		
		10p		
		11p		
		12p		
		1a		
		2a		
		3a		
		4a		

FOCUS 3 _____

Date _____ **FOCUS 1** _____

Sunday ___	Monday ___		Tuesday ___	Wednesday ___
		5a		
		6a		
		7a		
		8a		
		9a		
		10a		
		11a		
		12p		
		1p		
		2p		
		3p		
		4p		
		5p		
		6p		
		7p		
		8p		
		9p		
		10p		
		11p		
		12p		
		1a		
		2a		
		3a		
		4a		

FOCUS 2 _____

Thursday ____	Friday ____	T	Saturday ____	Notes
		5a		
		6a		
		7a		
		8a		
		9a		
		10a		
		11a		
		12p		
		1p		
		2p		
		3p		
		4p		
		5p		
		6p		
		7p		
		8p		
		9p		
		10p		
		11p		
		12p		
		1a		
		2a		
		3a		
		4a		

FOCUS 3 _____

Date _____ **FOCUS 1** _____

Sunday ___	Monday ___		Tuesday ___	Wednesday ___
		5a		
		6a		
		7a		
		8a		
		9a		
		10a		
		11a		
		12p		
		1p		
		2p		
		3p		
		4p		
		5p		
		6p		
		7p		
		8p		
		9p		
		10p		
		11p		
		12p		
		1a		
		2a		
		3a		
		4a		

FOCUS 2 _____

Thursday ___	Friday ___	T	Saturday ___	Notes
		5a		
		6a		
		7a		
		8a		
		9a		
		10a		
		11a		
		12p		
		1p		
		2p		
		3p		
		4p		
		5p		
		6p		
		7p		
		8p		
		9p		
		10p		
		11p		
		12p		
		1a		
		2a		
		3a		
		4a		

FOCUS 3 _____

	Week 1				Week 2	
Goal 1	**Goal 2**	**Goal 3**		**Goal 1**	**Goal 2**	**Goal 3**
			1			
			2			
			3			
			4			
			5			
			6			
			7			
			8			
			9			
			10			
			11			
			12			

Pick 1 - 3 Weekly Goals. These may relate to your yearly goals or be smaller.
Write the goal in step 1 and then each task required to complete it. Complete tasks during the week.

Week 3

Goal 1	Goal 2	Goal 3

Week 4

Goal 1	Goal 2	Goal 3

1
2
3
4
5
6
7
8
9
10
11
12

Date _____		FOCUS 1 _____		
Sunday ___	**Monday** ___		**Tuesday** ___	**Wednesday** ___
		5a		
		6a		
		7a		
		8a		
		9a		
		10a		
		11a		
		12p		
		1p		
		2p		
		3p		
		4p		
		5p		
		6p		
		7p		
		8p		
		9p		
		10p		
		11p		
		12p		
		1a		
		2a		
		3a		
		4a		

FOCUS 2 _____

	Thursday___	Friday___	T	Saturday___	Notes
			5a		
			6a		
			7a		
			8a		
			9a		
			10a		
			11a		
			12p		
			1p		
			2p		
			3p		
			4p		
			5p		
			6p		
			7p		
			8p		
			9p		
			10p		
			11p		
			12p		
			1a		
			2a		
			3a		
			4a		

FOCUS 3 _____

| Date _____ | | FOCUS 1 _____ | |
Sunday ___	Monday ___		Tuesday ___	Wednesday ___
		5a		
		6a		
		7a		
		8a		
		9a		
		10a		
		11a		
		12p		
		1p		
		2p		
		3p		
		4p		
		5p		
		6p		
		7p		
		8p		
		9p		
		10p		
		11p		
		12p		
		1a		
		2a		
		3a		
		4a		

Thursday ___	Friday ___	T	Saturday ___	Notes
		5a		
		6a		
		7a		
		8a		
		9a		
		10a		
		11a		
		12p		
		1p		
		2p		
		3p		
		4p		
		5p		
		6p		
		7p		
		8p		
		9p		
		10p		
		11p		
		12p		
		1a		
		2a		
		3a		
		4a		

Date _____	FOCUS 1 _____

Sunday ____	Monday ____		Tuesday ____	Wednesday ____
		5a		
		6a		
		7a		
		8a		
		9a		
		10a		
		11a		
		12p		
		1p		
		2p		
		3p		
		4p		
		5p		
		6p		
		7p		
		8p		
		9p		
		10p		
		11p		
		12p		
		1a		
		2a		
		3a		
		4a		

FOCUS 2 _____

Thursday____	Friday____	T	FOCUS 3 _____ Saturday____	Notes
		5a		
		6a		
		7a		
		8a		
		9a		
		10a		
		11a		
		12p		
		1p		
		2p		
		3p		
		4p		
		5p		
		6p		
		7p		
		8p		
		9p		
		10p		
		11p		
		12p		
		1a		
		2a		
		3a		
		4a		

Sunday ___	Monday ___		Tuesday ___	Wednesday ___
		5a		
		6a		
		7a		
		8a		
		9a		
		10a		
		11a		
		12p		
		1p		
		2p		
		3p		
		4p		
		5p		
		6p		
		7p		
		8p		
		9p		
		10p		
		11p		
		12p		
		1a		
		2a		
		3a		
		4a		

FOCUS 2 _____

Thursday____	Friday____	T	Saturday____	Notes
		5a		
		6a		
		7a		
		8a		
		9a		
		10a		
		11a		
		12p		
		1p		
		2p		
		3p		
		4p		
		5p		
		6p		
		7p		
		8p		
		9p		
		10p		
		11p		
		12p		
		1a		
		2a		
		3a		
		4a		

FOCUS 3 _____

Monthly Planning 3   Month _____   Year _____

Week 1				Week 2		
Goal 1	Goal 2	Goal 3		Goal 1	Goal 2	Goal 3
			1			
			2			
			3			
			4			
			5			
			6			
			7			
			8			
			9			
			10			
			11			
			12			

Pick 1 - 3 Weekly Goals. These may relate to your yearly goals or be smaller.
Write the goal in step 1 and then each task required to complete it. Complete tasks during the week.

Week 3				Week 4		
Goal 1	**Goal 2**	**Goal 3**		**Goal 1**	**Goal 2**	**Goal 3**
			1			
			2			
			3			
			4			
			5			
			6			
			7			
			8			
			9			
			10			
			11			
			12			

Date _____ FOCUS 1 _____

Sunday ____	Monday ____		Tuesday ____	Wednesday ____
		5a		
		6a		
		7a		
		8a		
		9a		
		10a		
		11a		
		12p		
		1p		
		2p		
		3p		
		4p		
		5p		
		6p		
		7p		
		8p		
		9p		
		10p		
		11p		
		12p		
		1a		
		2a		
		3a		
		4a		

Perry The Inventor's® World's Best Selling Time Blocking Planner

Thursday	Friday	T	Saturday	Notes
		5a		
		6a		
		7a		
		8a		
		9a		
		10a		
		11a		
		12p		
		1p		
		2p		
		3p		
		4p		
		5p		
		6p		
		7p		
		8p		
		9p		
		10p		
		11p		
		12p		
		1a		
		2a		
		3a		
		4a		

Date _____ FOCUS 1 _____

Sunday ____	Monday ____		Tuesday ____	Wednesday ____
		5a		
		6a		
		7a		
		8a		
		9a		
		10a		
		11a		
		12p		
		1p		
		2p		
		3p		
		4p		
		5p		
		6p		
		7p		
		8p		
		9p		
		10p		
		11p		
		12p		
		1a		
		2a		
		3a		
		4a		

FOCUS 2 _____

Thursday___	Friday___	T	Saturday___	Notes
		5a		
		6a		
		7a		
		8a		
		9a		
		10a		
		11a		
		12p		
		1p		
		2p		
		3p		
		4p		
		5p		
		6p		
		7p		
		8p		
		9p		
		10p		
		11p		
		12p		
		1a		
		2a		
		3a		
		4a		

FOCUS 3 _____

FOCUS 1 _____

Sunday ____	Monday ____		Tuesday ____	Wednesday ____
		5a		
		6a		
		7a		
		8a		
		9a		
		10a		
		11a		
		12p		
		1p		
		2p		
		3p		
		4p		
		5p		
		6p		
		7p		
		8p		
		9p		
		10p		
		11p		
		12p		
		1a		
		2a		
		3a		
		4a		

FOCUS 2 _____
Thursday ___	Friday ___	T	Saturday ___	Notes
		5a		
		6a		
		7a		
		8a		
		9a		
		10a		
		11a		
		12p		
		1p		
		2p		
		3p		
		4p		
		5p		
		6p		
		7p		
		8p		
		9p		
		10p		
		11p		
		12p		
		1a		
		2a		
		3a		
		4a		

FOCUS 3 _____

Date _____		FOCUS 1 _____	
Sunday ___	**Monday** ___	**Tuesday** ___	**Wednesday** ___
		5a		
		6a		
		7a		
		8a		
		9a		
		10a		
		11a		
		12p		
		1p		
		2p		
		3p		
		4p		
		5p		
		6p		
		7p		
		8p		
		9p		
		10p		
		11p		
		12p		
		1a		
		2a		
		3a		
		4a		

FOCUS 2 ____________________

FOCUS 3 ____________________

Thursday ___	Friday ___	T	Saturday ___	Notes
		5a		
		6a		
		7a		
		8a		
		9a		
		10a		
		11a		
		12p		
		1p		
		2p		
		3p		
		4p		
		5p		
		6p		
		7p		
		8p		
		9p		
		10p		
		11p		
		12p		
		1a		
		2a		
		3a		
		4a		

Monthly Planning 4   Month _____   Year _____

Week 1				Week 2		
Goal 1	**Goal 2**	**Goal 3**		**Goal 1**	**Goal 2**	**Goal 3**
			1			
			2			
			3			
			4			
			5			
			6			
			7			
			8			
			9			
			10			
			11			
			12			

Pick 1 - 3 Weekly Goals. These may relate to your yearly goals or be smaller.
Write the goal in step 1 and then each task required to complete it. Complete tasks during the week.

Week 3				Week 4		
Goal 1	**Goal 2**	**Goal 3**		**Goal 1**	**Goal 2**	**Goal 3**
			1			
			2			
			3			
			4			
			5			
			6			
			7			
			8			
			9			
			10			
			11			
			12			

Sunday ___	Monday ___		Tuesday ___	Wednesday ___
		5a		
		6a		
		7a		
		8a		
		9a		
		10a		
		11a		
		12p		
		1p		
		2p		
		3p		
		4p		
		5p		
		6p		
		7p		
		8p		
		9p		
		10p		
		11p		
		12p		
		1a		
		2a		
		3a		
		4a		

FOCUS 2 _____

Thursday ___	Friday ___	T	Saturday ___	Notes
		5a		
		6a		
		7a		
		8a		
		9a		
		10a		
		11a		
		12p		
		1p		
		2p		
		3p		
		4p		
		5p		
		6p		
		7p		
		8p		
		9p		
		10p		
		11p		
		12p		
		1a		
		2a		
		3a		
		4a		

FOCUS 3 _____

Date _____		FOCUS 1 _____		
Sunday ___	**Monday** ___		**Tuesday** ___	**Wednesday** ___
		5a		
		6a		
		7a		
		8a		
		9a		
		10a		
		11a		
		12p		
		1p		
		2p		
		3p		
		4p		
		5p		
		6p		
		7p		
		8p		
		9p		
		10p		
		11p		
		12p		
		1a		
		2a		
		3a		
		4a		

FOCUS 2 _____

Thursday ___	Friday ___	T	Saturday ___	Notes
		5a		
		6a		
		7a		
		8a		
		9a		
		10a		
		11a		
		12p		
		1p		
		2p		
		3p		
		4p		
		5p		
		6p		
		7p		
		8p		
		9p		
		10p		
		11p		
		12p		
		1a		
		2a		
		3a		
		4a		

FOCUS 3 _____

Date _____ **FOCUS 1** _____

Sunday ___	Monday ___		Tuesday ___	Wednesday ___
		5a		
		6a		
		7a		
		8a		
		9a		
		10a		
		11a		
		12p		
		1p		
		2p		
		3p		
		4p		
		5p		
		6p		
		7p		
		8p		
		9p		
		10p		
		11p		
		12p		
		1a		
		2a		
		3a		
		4a		

Thursday ___	Friday ___	T	Saturday ___	Notes
		5a		
		6a		
		7a		
		8a		
		9a		
		10a		
		11a		
		12p		
		1p		
		2p		
		3p		
		4p		
		5p		
		6p		
		7p		
		8p		
		9p		
		10p		
		11p		
		12p		
		1a		
		2a		
		3a		
		4a		

Date _____ FOCUS 1 _____

Sunday____	Monday____		Tuesday____	Wednesday____
		5a		
		6a		
		7a		
		8a		
		9a		
		10a		
		11a		
		12p		
		1p		
		2p		
		3p		
		4p		
		5p		
		6p		
		7p		
		8p		
		9p		
		10p		
		11p		
		12p		
		1a		
		2a		
		3a		
		4a		

Perry The Inventor's® World's Best Selling Time Blocking Planner

Thursday ___	Friday ___	T	Saturday ___	Notes
		5a		
		6a		
		7a		
		8a		
		9a		
		10a		
		11a		
		12p		
		1p		
		2p		
		3p		
		4p		
		5p		
		6p		
		7p		
		8p		
		9p		
		10p		
		11p		
		12p		
		1a		
		2a		
		3a		
		4a		

Monthly Planning 5   Month _____   Year _____

	Week 1				Week 2	
Goal 1	**Goal 2**	**Goal 3**		**Goal 1**	**Goal 2**	**Goal 3**
			1			
			2			
			3			
			4			
			5			
			6			
			7			
			8			
			9			
			10			
			11			
			12			

Pick 1 - 3 Weekly Goals. These may relate to your yearly goals or be smaller.
Write the goal in step 1 and then each task required to complete it. Complete tasks during the week.

Week 3				Week 4		
Goal 1	Goal 2	Goal 3		Goal 1	Goal 2	Goal 3
			1			
			2			
			3			
			4			
			5			
			6			
			7			
			8			
			9			
			10			
			11			
			12			

Date _____		FOCUS 1 _____	
Sunday ____	**Monday** ____	**Tuesday** ____	**Wednesday** ____
		5a	
		6a	
		7a	
		8a	
		9a	
		10a	
		11a	
		12p	
		1p	
		2p	
		3p	
		4p	
		5p	
		6p	
		7p	
		8p	
		9p	
		10p	
		11p	
		12p	
		1a	
		2a	
		3a	
		4a	

FOCUS 2 _____

FOCUS 3 _____

Thursday ____	Friday ____	T	Saturday ____	Notes
		5a		
		6a		
		7a		
		8a		
		9a		
		10a		
		11a		
		12p		
		1p		
		2p		
		3p		
		4p		
		5p		
		6p		
		7p		
		8p		
		9p		
		10p		
		11p		
		12p		
		1a		
		2a		
		3a		
		4a		

Sunday ___	Monday ___		Tuesday ___	Wednesday ___
		5a		
		6a		
		7a		
		8a		
		9a		
		10a		
		11a		
		12p		
		1p		
		2p		
		3p		
		4p		
		5p		
		6p		
		7p		
		8p		
		9p		
		10p		
		11p		
		12p		
		1a		
		2a		
		3a		
		4a		

Thursday ___	Friday ___	T	Saturday ___	Notes
		5a		
		6a		
		7a		
		8a		
		9a		
		10a		
		11a		
		12p		
		1p		
		2p		
		3p		
		4p		
		5p		
		6p		
		7p		
		8p		
		9p		
		10p		
		11p		
		12p		
		1a		
		2a		
		3a		
		4a		

Date _____		FOCUS 1 _____	
Sunday ___	**Monday** ___		**Tuesday** ___	**Wednesday** ___
		5a		
		6a		
		7a		
		8a		
		9a		
		10a		
		11a		
		12p		
		1p		
		2p		
		3p		
		4p		
		5p		
		6p		
		7p		
		8p		
		9p		
		10p		
		11p		
		12p		
		1a		
		2a		
		3a		
		4a		

Thursday ___	Friday ___	T	Saturday ___	Notes
		5a		
		6a		
		7a		
		8a		
		9a		
		10a		
		11a		
		12p		
		1p		
		2p		
		3p		
		4p		
		5p		
		6p		
		7p		
		8p		
		9p		
		10p		
		11p		
		12p		
		1a		
		2a		
		3a		
		4a		

Sunday____	Monday____		Tuesday____	Wednesday____
		5a		
		6a		
		7a		
		8a		
		9a		
		10a		
		11a		
		12p		
		1p		
		2p		
		3p		
		4p		
		5p		
		6p		
		7p		
		8p		
		9p		
		10p		
		11p		
		12p		
		1a		
		2a		
		3a		
		4a		

FOCUS 2 _____
Thursday ____   Friday ____

FOCUS 3 _____
Saturday ____   Notes

Thursday	Friday	T	Saturday	Notes
		5a		
		6a		
		7a		
		8a		
		9a		
		10a		
		11a		
		12p		
		1p		
		2p		
		3p		
		4p		
		5p		
		6p		
		7p		
		8p		
		9p		
		10p		
		11p		
		12p		
		1a		
		2a		
		3a		
		4a		

Monthly Planning 6   Month _____   Year _____

Week 1				Week 2		
Goal 1	**Goal 2**	**Goal 3**		**Goal 1**	**Goal 2**	**Goal 3**
			1			
			2			
			3			
			4			
			5			
			6			
			7			
			8			
			9			
			10			
			11			
			12			

Pick 1 - 3 Weekly Goals. These may relate to your yearly goals or be smaller.
Write the goal in step 1 and then each task required to complete it. Complete tasks during the week.

Week 3

Goal 1	Goal 2	Goal 3

Week 4

Goal 1	Goal 2	Goal 3

1
2
3
4
5
6
7
8
9
10
11
12

Date _____ FOCUS 1 _____

Sunday ___	Monday ___		Tuesday ___	Wednesday ___
		5a		
		6a		
		7a		
		8a		
		9a		
		10a		
		11a		
		12p		
		1p		
		2p		
		3p		
		4p		
		5p		
		6p		
		7p		
		8p		
		9p		
		10p		
		11p		
		12p		
		1a		
		2a		
		3a		
		4a		

FOCUS 2 _____

	Thursday ____	Friday ____	T	Saturday ____	Notes
			5a		
			6a		
			7a		
			8a		
			9a		
			10a		
			11a		
			12p		
			1p		
			2p		
			3p		
			4p		
			5p		
			6p		
			7p		
			8p		
			9p		
			10p		
			11p		
			12p		
			1a		
			2a		
			3a		
			4a		

FOCUS 3 _____

Sunday ___	Monday ___		Tuesday ___	Wednesday ___
		5a		
		6a		
		7a		
		8a		
		9a		
		10a		
		11a		
		12p		
		1p		
		2p		
		3p		
		4p		
		5p		
		6p		
		7p		
		8p		
		9p		
		10p		
		11p		
		12p		
		1a		
		2a		
		3a		
		4a		

Thursday	Friday	T	Saturday	Notes
		5a		
		6a		
		7a		
		8a		
		9a		
		10a		
		11a		
		12p		
		1p		
		2p		
		3p		
		4p		
		5p		
		6p		
		7p		
		8p		
		9p		
		10p		
		11p		
		12p		
		1a		
		2a		
		3a		
		4a		

Date _____		FOCUS 1 _____		
Sunday ___	**Monday** ___		**Tuesday** ___	**Wednesday** ___
		5a		
		6a		
		7a		
		8a		
		9a		
		10a		
		11a		
		12p		
		1p		
		2p		
		3p		
		4p		
		5p		
		6p		
		7p		
		8p		
		9p		
		10p		
		11p		
		12p		
		1a		
		2a		
		3a		
		4a		

FOCUS 2 _____

Thursday ____	Friday ____	T	FOCUS 3 _____ Saturday ____	Notes
		5a		
		6a		
		7a		
		8a		
		9a		
		10a		
		11a		
		12p		
		1p		
		2p		
		3p		
		4p		
		5p		
		6p		
		7p		
		8p		
		9p		
		10p		
		11p		
		12p		
		1a		
		2a		
		3a		
		4a		

Sunday___	Monday___		Tuesday___	Wednesday___
		5a		
		6a		
		7a		
		8a		
		9a		
		10a		
		11a		
		12p		
		1p		
		2p		
		3p		
		4p		
		5p		
		6p		
		7p		
		8p		
		9p		
		10p		
		11p		
		12p		
		1a		
		2a		
		3a		
		4a		

Thursday	Friday	T	Saturday	Notes
		5a		
		6a		
		7a		
		8a		
		9a		
		10a		
		11a		
		12p		
		1p		
		2p		
		3p		
		4p		
		5p		
		6p		
		7p		
		8p		
		9p		
		10p		
		11p		
		12p		
		1a		
		2a		
		3a		
		4a		

Monthly Planning 7

Month _____   Year _____

	Week 1				Week 2	
Goal 1	**Goal 2**	**Goal 3**		**Goal 1**	**Goal 2**	**Goal 3**
			1			
			2			
			3			
			4			
			5			
			6			
			7			
			8			
			9			
			10			
			11			
			12			

Perry The Inventor's® World's Best Selling Time Blocking Planner

Pick 1 - 3 Weekly Goals. These may relate to your yearly goals or be smaller.
Write the goal in step 1 and then each task required to complete it. Complete tasks during the week.

Week 3				Week 4		
Goal 1	Goal 2	Goal 3		Goal 1	Goal 2	Goal 3
			1			
			2			
			3			
			4			
			5			
			6			
			7			
			8			
			9			
			10			
			11			
			12			

Sunday ___	Monday ___		Tuesday ___	Wednesday ___
		5a		
		6a		
		7a		
		8a		
		9a		
		10a		
		11a		
		12p		
		1p		
		2p		
		3p		
		4p		
		5p		
		6p		
		7p		
		8p		
		9p		
		10p		
		11p		
		12p		
		1a		
		2a		
		3a		
		4a		

Thursday____	Friday____	T	Saturday____	Notes
		5a		
		6a		
		7a		
		8a		
		9a		
		10a		
		11a		
		12p		
		1p		
		2p		
		3p		
		4p		
		5p		
		6p		
		7p		
		8p		
		9p		
		10p		
		11p		
		12p		
		1a		
		2a		
		3a		
		4a		

Sunday ___	Monday ___		Tuesday ___	Wednesday ___
		5a		
		6a		
		7a		
		8a		
		9a		
		10a		
		11a		
		12p		
		1p		
		2p		
		3p		
		4p		
		5p		
		6p		
		7p		
		8p		
		9p		
		10p		
		11p		
		12p		
		1a		
		2a		
		3a		
		4a		

Thursday___	Friday___	T	Saturday___	Notes
		5a		
		6a		
		7a		
		8a		
		9a		
		10a		
		11a		
		12p		
		1p		
		2p		
		3p		
		4p		
		5p		
		6p		
		7p		
		8p		
		9p		
		10p		
		11p		
		12p		
		1a		
		2a		
		3a		
		4a		

Sunday ___	Monday ___		Tuesday ___	Wednesday ___
		5a		
		6a		
		7a		
		8a		
		9a		
		10a		
		11a		
		12p		
		1p		
		2p		
		3p		
		4p		
		5p		
		6p		
		7p		
		8p		
		9p		
		10p		
		11p		
		12p		
		1a		
		2a		
		3a		
		4a		

Thursday ___	Friday ___	T	Saturday ___	Notes
		5a		
		6a		
		7a		
		8a		
		9a		
		10a		
		11a		
		12p		
		1p		
		2p		
		3p		
		4p		
		5p		
		6p		
		7p		
		8p		
		9p		
		10p		
		11p		
		12p		
		1a		
		2a		
		3a		
		4a		

Date _____ FOCUS 1 _____

Sunday ___	Monday ___		Tuesday ___	Wednesday ___
		5a		
		6a		
		7a		
		8a		
		9a		
		10a		
		11a		
		12p		
		1p		
		2p		
		3p		
		4p		
		5p		
		6p		
		7p		
		8p		
		9p		
		10p		
		11p		
		12p		
		1a		
		2a		
		3a		
		4a		

Thursday____	Friday____	T	Saturday____	Notes
		5a		
		6a		
		7a		
		8a		
		9a		
		10a		
		11a		
		12p		
		1p		
		2p		
		3p		
		4p		
		5p		
		6p		
		7p		
		8p		
		9p		
		10p		
		11p		
		12p		
		1a		
		2a		
		3a		
		4a		

Monthly Planning 8   Month _____   Year _____

Week 1				Week 2		
Goal 1	**Goal 2**	**Goal 3**		**Goal 1**	**Goal 2**	**Goal 3**
			1			
			2			
			3			
			4			
			5			
			6			
			7			
			8			
			9			
			10			
			11			
			12			

Pick 1 - 3 Weekly Goals. These may relate to your yearly goals or be smaller.
Write the goal in step 1 and then each task required to complete it. Complete tasks during the week.

Week 3

Goal 1	Goal 2	Goal 3

1
2
3
4
5
6
7
8
9
10
11
12

Week 4

Goal 1	Goal 2	Goal 3

Date _____			FOCUS 1 _____	
Sunday ____	**Monday** ____		**Tuesday** ____	**Wednesday** ____
		5a		
		6a		
		7a		
		8a		
		9a		
		10a		
		11a		
		12p		
		1p		
		2p		
		3p		
		4p		
		5p		
		6p		
		7p		
		8p		
		9p		
		10p		
		11p		
		12p		
		1a		
		2a		
		3a		
		4a		

FOCUS 2 _____

Thursday ____	Friday ____	T	Saturday ____	Notes
		5a		
		6a		
		7a		
		8a		
		9a		
		10a		
		11a		
		12p		
		1p		
		2p		
		3p		
		4p		
		5p		
		6p		
		7p		
		8p		
		9p		
		10p		
		11p		
		12p		
		1a		
		2a		
		3a		
		4a		

FOCUS 3 _____

Sunday ___	Monday ___		Tuesday ___	Wednesday ___
		5a		
		6a		
		7a		
		8a		
		9a		
		10a		
		11a		
		12p		
		1p		
		2p		
		3p		
		4p		
		5p		
		6p		
		7p		
		8p		
		9p		
		10p		
		11p		
		12p		
		1a		
		2a		
		3a		
		4a		

Thursday___	Friday___	T	Saturday___	Notes
		5a		
		6a		
		7a		
		8a		
		9a		
		10a		
		11a		
		12p		
		1p		
		2p		
		3p		
		4p		
		5p		
		6p		
		7p		
		8p		
		9p		
		10p		
		11p		
		12p		
		1a		
		2a		
		3a		
		4a		

Sunday ___	Monday ___		Tuesday ___	Wednesday ___
		5a		
		6a		
		7a		
		8a		
		9a		
		10a		
		11a		
		12p		
		1p		
		2p		
		3p		
		4p		
		5p		
		6p		
		7p		
		8p		
		9p		
		10p		
		11p		
		12p		
		1a		
		2a		
		3a		
		4a		

FOCUS 2 _____

Thursday____	Friday____	T	Saturday____	Notes
		5a		
		6a		
		7a		
		8a		
		9a		
		10a		
		11a		
		12p		
		1p		
		2p		
		3p		
		4p		
		5p		
		6p		
		7p		
		8p		
		9p		
		10p		
		11p		
		12p		
		1a		
		2a		
		3a		
		4a		

FOCUS 3 _____

	Date _____		FOCUS 1 _____	
	Sunday ___	**Monday** ___		**Tuesday** ___	**Wednesday** ___
5a				
6a				
7a				
8a				
9a				
10a				
11a				
12p				
1p				
2p				
3p				
4p				
5p				
6p				
7p				
8p				
9p				
10p				
11p				
12p				
1a				
2a				
3a				
4a				

Thursday ___	Friday ___	T	Saturday ___	Notes
		5a		
		6a		
		7a		
		8a		
		9a		
		10a		
		11a		
		12p		
		1p		
		2p		
		3p		
		4p		
		5p		
		6p		
		7p		
		8p		
		9p		
		10p		
		11p		
		12p		
		1a		
		2a		
		3a		
		4a		

Month _____ **Year** _____

	Week 1			Week 2	
Goal 1	Goal 2	Goal 3	Goal 1	Goal 2	Goal 3

1
2
3
4
5
6
7
8
9
10
11
12

Pick 1 - 3 Weekly Goals. These may relate to your yearly goals or be smaller.
Write the goal in step 1 and then each task required to complete it. Complete tasks during the week.

Week 3				Week 4		
Goal 1	**Goal 2**	**Goal 3**		**Goal 1**	**Goal 2**	**Goal 3**
			1			
			2			
			3			
			4			
			5			
			6			
			7			
			8			
			9			
			10			
			11			
			12			

Sunday ____	Monday ____		Tuesday ____	Wednesday ____
		5a		
		6a		
		7a		
		8a		
		9a		
		10a		
		11a		
		12p		
		1p		
		2p		
		3p		
		4p		
		5p		
		6p		
		7p		
		8p		
		9p		
		10p		
		11p		
		12p		
		1a		
		2a		
		3a		
		4a		

	Thursday ____	Friday ____	T	Saturday ____	Notes
			5a		
			6a		
			7a		
			8a		
			9a		
			10a		
			11a		
			12p		
			1p		
			2p		
			3p		
			4p		
			5p		
			6p		
			7p		
			8p		
			9p		
			10p		
			11p		
			12p		
			1a		
			2a		
			3a		
			4a		

Date _____   FOCUS 1 _____

Sunday ____	Monday ____		Tuesday ____	Wednesday ____
		5a		
		6a		
		7a		
		8a		
		9a		
		10a		
		11a		
		12p		
		1p		
		2p		
		3p		
		4p		
		5p		
		6p		
		7p		
		8p		
		9p		
		10p		
		11p		
		12p		
		1a		
		2a		
		3a		
		4a		

Thursday ___	Friday ___	T	Saturday ___	Notes
		5a		
		6a		
		7a		
		8a		
		9a		
		10a		
		11a		
		12p		
		1p		
		2p		
		3p		
		4p		
		5p		
		6p		
		7p		
		8p		
		9p		
		10p		
		11p		
		12p		
		1a		
		2a		
		3a		
		4a		

Sunday ___	Monday ___		Tuesday ___	Wednesday ___
		5a		
		6a		
		7a		
		8a		
		9a		
		10a		
		11a		
		12p		
		1p		
		2p		
		3p		
		4p		
		5p		
		6p		
		7p		
		8p		
		9p		
		10p		
		11p		
		12p		
		1a		
		2a		
		3a		
		4a		

Thursday ___	Friday ___	T	Saturday ___	Notes
		5a		
		6a		
		7a		
		8a		
		9a		
		10a		
		11a		
		12p		
		1p		
		2p		
		3p		
		4p		
		5p		
		6p		
		7p		
		8p		
		9p		
		10p		
		11p		
		12p		
		1a		
		2a		
		3a		
		4a		

Sunday ___	Monday ___			Tuesday ___	Wednesday ___
		5a			
		6a			
		7a			
		8a			
		9a			
		10a			
		11a			
		12p			
		1p			
		2p			
		3p			
		4p			
		5p			
		6p			
		7p			
		8p			
		9p			
		10p			
		11p			
		12p			
		1a			
		2a			
		3a			
		4a			

FOCUS 2 _____

Thursday____	Friday____	T	Saturday____	Notes
		5a		
		6a		
		7a		
		8a		
		9a		
		10a		
		11a		
		12p		
		1p		
		2p		
		3p		
		4p		
		5p		
		6p		
		7p		
		8p		
		9p		
		10p		
		11p		
		12p		
		1a		
		2a		
		3a		
		4a		

FOCUS 3 _____

Monthly Planning 10   Month _____   Year _____

	Week 1				Week 2	
Goal 1	**Goal 2**	**Goal 3**		**Goal 1**	**Goal 2**	**Goal 3**
			1			
			2			
			3			
			4			
			5			
			6			
			7			
			8			
			9			
			10			
			11			
			12			

Pick 1 - 3 Weekly Goals. These may relate to your yearly goals or be smaller.
Write the goal in step 1 and then each task required to complete it. Complete tasks during the week.

Week 3

Goal 1	Goal 2	Goal 3

Week 4

Goal 1	Goal 2	Goal 3

1
2
3
4
5
6
7
8
9
10
11
12

Sunday ___	Monday ___		Tuesday ___	Wednesday ___
		Date ___ **FOCUS 1** ___		
		5a		
		6a		
		7a		
		8a		
		9a		
		10a		
		11a		
		12p		
		1p		
		2p		
		3p		
		4p		
		5p		
		6p		
		7p		
		8p		
		9p		
		10p		
		11p		
		12p		
		1a		
		2a		
		3a		
		4a		

FOCUS 2 _____

Thursday ____	Friday ____	T	Saturday ____	Notes
		5a		
		6a		
		7a		
		8a		
		9a		
		10a		
		11a		
		12p		
		1p		
		2p		
		3p		
		4p		
		5p		
		6p		
		7p		
		8p		
		9p		
		10p		
		11p		
		12p		
		1a		
		2a		
		3a		
		4a		

FOCUS 3 _____

Sunday ___	Monday ___		Tuesday ___	Wednesday ___
		5a		
		6a		
		7a		
		8a		
		9a		
		10a		
		11a		
		12p		
		1p		
		2p		
		3p		
		4p		
		5p		
		6p		
		7p		
		8p		
		9p		
		10p		
		11p		
		12p		
		1a		
		2a		
		3a		
		4a		

Thursday ___	Friday ___	T	Saturday ___	Notes
		5a		
		6a		
		7a		
		8a		
		9a		
		10a		
		11a		
		12p		
		1p		
		2p		
		3p		
		4p		
		5p		
		6p		
		7p		
		8p		
		9p		
		10p		
		11p		
		12p		
		1a		
		2a		
		3a		
		4a		

Date _____			FOCUS 1 _____		
Sunday ___	**Monday** ___		**Tuesday** ___	**Wednesday** ___
		5a		
		6a		
		7a		
		8a		
		9a		
		10a		
		11a		
		12p		
		1p		
		2p		
		3p		
		4p		
		5p		
		6p		
		7p		
		8p		
		9p		
		10p		
		11p		
		12p		
		1a		
		2a		
		3a		
		4a		

FOCUS 2 _____

Thursday ___	Friday ___	T	FOCUS 3 _____ Saturday ___	Notes
		5a		
		6a		
		7a		
		8a		
		9a		
		10a		
		11a		
		12p		
		1p		
		2p		
		3p		
		4p		
		5p		
		6p		
		7p		
		8p		
		9p		
		10p		
		11p		
		12p		
		1a		
		2a		
		3a		
		4a		

Date _____ FOCUS 1 _____

Sunday ___	Monday ___		Tuesday ___	Wednesday ___
		5a		
		6a		
		7a		
		8a		
		9a		
		10a		
		11a		
		12p		
		1p		
		2p		
		3p		
		4p		
		5p		
		6p		
		7p		
		8p		
		9p		
		10p		
		11p		
		12p		
		1a		
		2a		
		3a		
		4a		

FOCUS 2 _____

Thursday____	Friday____	T	Saturday____	Notes
		5a		
		6a		
		7a		
		8a		
		9a		
		10a		
		11a		
		12p		
		1p		
		2p		
		3p		
		4p		
		5p		
		6p		
		7p		
		8p		
		9p		
		10p		
		11p		
		12p		
		1a		
		2a		
		3a		
		4a		

FOCUS 3 _____

Monthly Planning 11

Month _____ **Year** _____

	Week 1				Week 2	
Goal 1	**Goal 2**	**Goal 3**		**Goal 1**	**Goal 2**	**Goal 3**
			1			
			2			
			3			
			4			
			5			
			6			
			7			
			8			
			9			
			10			
			11			
			12			

Pick 1 - 3 Weekly Goals. These may relate to your yearly goals or be smaller.
Write the goal in step 1 and then each task required to complete it. Complete tasks during the week.

Week 3				Week 4		
Goal 1	**Goal 2**	**Goal 3**		**Goal 1**	**Goal 2**	**Goal 3**
			1			
			2			
			3			
			4			
			5			
			6			
			7			
			8			
			9			
			10			
			11			
			12			

Sunday____	Monday____		Tuesday____	Wednesday____
		5a		
		6a		
		7a		
		8a		
		9a		
		10a		
		11a		
		12p		
		1p		
		2p		
		3p		
		4p		
		5p		
		6p		
		7p		
		8p		
		9p		
		10p		
		11p		
		12p		
		1a		
		2a		
		3a		
		4a		

Thursday	Friday	T	Saturday	Notes
		5a		
		6a		
		7a		
		8a		
		9a		
		10a		
		11a		
		12p		
		1p		
		2p		
		3p		
		4p		
		5p		
		6p		
		7p		
		8p		
		9p		
		10p		
		11p		
		12p		
		1a		
		2a		
		3a		
		4a		

Date _____ FOCUS 1 _____

Sunday ___	Monday ___		Tuesday ___	Wednesday ___
		5a		
		6a		
		7a		
		8a		
		9a		
		10a		
		11a		
		12p		
		1p		
		2p		
		3p		
		4p		
		5p		
		6p		
		7p		
		8p		
		9p		
		10p		
		11p		
		12p		
		1a		
		2a		
		3a		
		4a		

Perry The Inventor's® World's Best Selling Time Blocking Planner

FOCUS 2 _____
Thursday ____   Friday ____

FOCUS 3 _____
Saturday ____   Notes

Thursday	Friday	T	Saturday	Notes
		5a		
		6a		
		7a		
		8a		
		9a		
		10a		
		11a		
		12p		
		1p		
		2p		
		3p		
		4p		
		5p		
		6p		
		7p		
		8p		
		9p		
		10p		
		11p		
		12p		
		1a		
		2a		
		3a		
		4a		

Date _____ FOCUS 1 _____

Sunday ___	Monday ___		Tuesday ___	Wednesday___
		5a		
		6a		
		7a		
		8a		
		9a		
		10a		
		11a		
		12p		
		1p		
		2p		
		3p		
		4p		
		5p		
		6p		
		7p		
		8p		
		9p		
		10p		
		11p		
		12p		
		1a		
		2a		
		3a		
		4a		

FOCUS 2 _____

Thursday ___	Friday ___	T	FOCUS 3 _____ Saturday ___	Notes
		5a		
		6a		
		7a		
		8a		
		9a		
		10a		
		11a		
		12p		
		1p		
		2p		
		3p		
		4p		
		5p		
		6p		
		7p		
		8p		
		9p		
		10p		
		11p		
		12p		
		1a		
		2a		
		3a		
		4a		

Date _____ FOCUS 1 _____

Sunday ___	Monday ___		Tuesday ___	Wednesday ___
		5a		
		6a		
		7a		
		8a		
		9a		
		10a		
		11a		
		12p		
		1p		
		2p		
		3p		
		4p		
		5p		
		6p		
		7p		
		8p		
		9p		
		10p		
		11p		
		12p		
		1a		
		2a		
		3a		
		4a		

FOCUS 2 _____

Thursday___	Friday___	T	FOCUS 3 _____ Saturday___	Notes
		5a		
		6a		
		7a		
		8a		
		9a		
		10a		
		11a		
		12p		
		1p		
		2p		
		3p		
		4p		
		5p		
		6p		
		7p		
		8p		
		9p		
		10p		
		11p		
		12p		
		1a		
		2a		
		3a		
		4a		

Monthly Planning 12   Month _____   Year _____

	Week 1				Week 2	
Goal 1	**Goal 2**	**Goal 3**		**Goal 1**	**Goal 2**	**Goal 3**
			1			
			2			
			3			
			4			
			5			
			6			
			7			
			8			
			9			
			10			
			11			
			12			

Pick 1 - 3 Weekly Goals. These may relate to your yearly goals or be smaller.
Write the goal in step 1 and then each task required to complete it. Complete tasks during the week.

Week 3				Week 4		
Goal 1	**Goal 2**	**Goal 3**		**Goal 1**	**Goal 2**	**Goal 3**
			1			
			2			
			3			
			4			
			5			
			6			
			7			
			8			
			9			
			10			
			11			
			12			

Date _____			FOCUS 1 _____	
Sunday ___	**Monday** ___		**Tuesday** ___	**Wednesday** ___
		5a		
		6a		
		7a		
		8a		
		9a		
		10a		
		11a		
		12p		
		1p		
		2p		
		3p		
		4p		
		5p		
		6p		
		7p		
		8p		
		9p		
		10p		
		11p		
		12p		
		1a		
		2a		
		3a		
		4a		

FOCUS 2 _____

	Thursday____	Friday____	T		Saturday____	Notes
			5a			
			6a			
			7a			
			8a			
			9a			
			10a			
			11a			
			12p			
			1p			
			2p			
			3p			
			4p			
			5p			
			6p			
			7p			
			8p			
			9p			
			10p			
			11p			
			12p			
			1a			
			2a			
			3a			
			4a			

FOCUS 3 _____

Sunday ____	Monday ____		Tuesday ____	Wednesday ____
		5a		
		6a		
		7a		
		8a		
		9a		
		10a		
		11a		
		12p		
		1p		
		2p		
		3p		
		4p		
		5p		
		6p		
		7p		
		8p		
		9p		
		10p		
		11p		
		12p		
		1a		
		2a		
		3a		
		4a		

FOCUS 2 _____

Thursday ___	Friday ___	T	Saturday ___	Notes
		5a		
		6a		
		7a		
		8a		
		9a		
		10a		
		11a		
		12p		
		1p		
		2p		
		3p		
		4p		
		5p		
		6p		
		7p		
		8p		
		9p		
		10p		
		11p		
		12p		
		1a		
		2a		
		3a		
		4a		

FOCUS 3 _____

Date _____ FOCUS 1 _____

Sunday ___	Monday ___		Tuesday ___	Wednesday ___
		5a		
		6a		
		7a		
		8a		
		9a		
		10a		
		11a		
		12p		
		1p		
		2p		
		3p		
		4p		
		5p		
		6p		
		7p		
		8p		
		9p		
		10p		
		11p		
		12p		
		1a		
		2a		
		3a		
		4a		

Thursday ___	Friday ___	T	Saturday ___	Notes
		5a		
		6a		
		7a		
		8a		
		9a		
		10a		
		11a		
		12p		
		1p		
		2p		
		3p		
		4p		
		5p		
		6p		
		7p		
		8p		
		9p		
		10p		
		11p		
		12p		
		1a		
		2a		
		3a		
		4a		

	Date _____	FOCUS 1 _____		
	Sunday ____	**Monday** ____		**Tuesday** ____	**Wednesday** ____

Sunday	Monday		Tuesday	Wednesday
		5a		
		6a		
		7a		
		8a		
		9a		
		10a		
		11a		
		12p		
		1p		
		2p		
		3p		
		4p		
		5p		
		6p		
		7p		
		8p		
		9p		
		10p		
		11p		
		12p		
		1a		
		2a		
		3a		
		4a		

Perry The Inventor's® World's Best Selling Time Blocking Planner

Thursday	Friday	T	Saturday	Notes
		5a		
		6a		
		7a		
		8a		
		9a		
		10a		
		11a		
		12p		
		1p		
		2p		
		3p		
		4p		
		5p		
		6p		
		7p		
		8p		
		9p		
		10p		
		11p		
		12p		
		1a		
		2a		
		3a		
		4a		

Section Five
Notes & Ideas

Notes About _____

THANK YOU!

for additional innovative products visit us...

PerryTheInventor.com

www.ingramcontent.com/pod-product-compliance
Lightning Source LLC
Chambersburg PA
CBHW062001090426
42811CB00006B/1003